A Family Life Nature Series

The Gospel According to a DANDELION

By Terry & Jean McComb

Illustrations by Vera McMurdo

www.TEACHServices.com • (800) 367-1844

World rights reserved. Portions of this book may be photocopied for evangelistic purposes.

The author assumes full responsibility for the accuracy of all facts and quotations as cited in this book. The opinions expressed in this book are the author's personal views and interpretations, and do not necessarily reflect those of the publisher.

This book is provided with the understanding that the publisher is not engaged in giving spiritual, legal, medical, or other professional advice. If authoritative advice is needed, the reader should seek the counsel of a competent professional.

All rights reserved. No part of this publication may be reproduced, stored in a retrieval system, or transmitted in any form or by any means, except for brief quotations in printed reviews, without the prior permission of the publisher. Portions of this book may be photocopied for evangelistic purposes.

Copyright© 2023 Terry & Jean McComb
Copyright© 2023 TEACH Services, Inc.
ISBN-13: 978-1-4796-1234-5 (Paperback)
ISBN-13: 978-1-4796-1235-2 ((ePub)
Library of Congress Control Number: 2023936156

Any personal website addresses that the author included are managed by the author. TEACH Services is not responsible for the accuracy or permanency of any links.

Scripture taken from the New King James Version®. Copyright © 1982 by Thomas Nelson. Used by permission. All rights reserved. Italics omitted.

Illustrations by Vera McMurdo

This book is a multi-faceted/multi-learning style resource that combines a reading lesson, a character lesson, a science lesson, a Bible lesson, and an art lesson—all with a unifying and educational theme. It also has an outdoor activity for each lesson that the family can enjoy together. We recommend that the teacher/parent take the child outdoors and read the lesson with the child by a real dandelion plant. Let the child ask questions, then invite the child to come inside and color the picture to further fasten the lesson to their open mind.

Published by

TEACH Services, Inc.
PUBLISHING
www.TEACHServices.com • (800) 367-1844

Table of Contents

Page	Chapter	Nature Object	Text	Character Lesson
v	*Preface*			
6	Outdoor Classroom	Wildflowers	Matthew 6:28	Consider
8	A Fragrance of Love	A Weed	Matthew 5:10	Good for Evil
10	The Leaf of a Dandelion	Leaf	Luke 8:14	Priorities
12	A Daily Schedule	Bract and Blossom	Matthew 6:31	Daily Devotion
14	Unity	Floret	Romans 12:10	Harmony
16	The Dandelion's Root System	Root	Psalms 119:11	Memory
18	The Stem	Stem and Osmosis	Romans 12:21	Holy Spirit
20	Flexibility	Growth Style	Proverbs 9:7–9	Reproof
22	Unrelenting Effort	Early Spring Flower	2 Timothy 4:2, 3	Not Lazy
24	Magnified Beauty	Stamen	Ecclesiastes 3:11	Natural beauty
26	Character Beauty	Pollen	1 Corinthians 14:40	Order
28	Hidden Beauty	Pollen Magnified	1 Peter 3:3, 4	Inner Beauty
30	The Dormant Stage	Enclosed by Bract	Proverbs 18:24	Standing Alone
32	Spreading Seeds	Seed with Silk	Acts 1:8	Witnessing
34	Seed Determines the Harvest	Brown Seed	Galatians 6:7–9	Reap and Sow
36	Hidden Hooks	Silk	Ecclesiastes 12:14	Motive
38	The Cross	Seeds Gone	2 Corinthians 8:9	Self-denial
40	Service and Ministry	Insects on Blossom	Isaiah 39:4	Law and Service
42	Counterfeits	Similar Blossom	Proverbs 3:5, 6	Carefulness
44	Detecting a Counterfeit	Compared Blossom	1 Corinthians 10:31	Counterfeits
46	Endurance	Habitat	John 16:33	Overcoming
48	Seeing the Big Picture	God's Orchestration	John 1:3	Our Place
51	Creation Seminars			

Please Notice Carefully

The book in your hands is a multi-lesson teaching device that will involve the parent, grandparent, or teacher in a family-type activity in God's Outdoor Classroom.

Each page is a stand-alone lesson that is: 1) a reading lesson, 2) a character lesson, 3) a Bible lesson, 4) a science lesson, and 5) an art lesson (color the picture) per page.

Each lesson is created to have the parent/teacher take the child outside and share the lesson by the real object of nature under study. The lesson can be tailored either up or down, based on the child's level of experience and understanding. Later have them carefully color the art opposite the text. The Practical Project accomplished outside will awaken curiosity to desire to know the Creator Who made such a wonderful object of nature.

The art page may be photocopied for classroom use but not for resale.

This resource is excellent for Sunday/Sabbath school use or Boy/Girl Scout Club devotions. VBS leaders will find these lessons very useful. Also, pastors can use these in the children's story time in the worship service. Have the child color the picture while the pastor preaches, thus doubling the attention span of any child.

"God has shown His invisible attributes, His eternal power, and divine nature, clearly by what He has made. People are without an excuse for not glorifying God as Creator and giving Him gratitude and thanks" (Romans 1:20–21, McComb paraphrase).

ENJOY!!

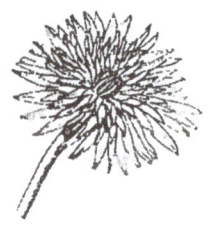

Preface

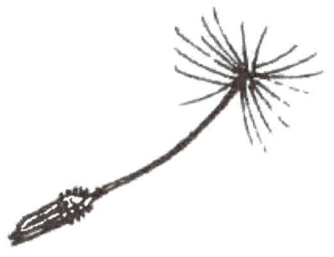

Parents and children are looking for ways to spend more time together. Nature's charm invites parents and children to explore its mysteries together. We encourage parents to read the lessons of this book to their children in the great out-of-doors classroom next to a real dandelion plant. If this is not possible, dig up a dandelion plant and put it in a pot and have it close for actual observation as you share the lesson indoors.

The focus of this book is on the character quality of endurance. As parents share these lessons they will be instilling this lasting quality into their child at the foundation level of development. "Here is the patience [endurance] of the saints: here are they that keep the commandments of God, and have the faith of Jesus" (Revelation 12:17).

After the lesson is shared the child may wish to color the picture. May this yellow wayside blossom charm your family with its quiet humble message, "God is still love."

Outdoor Classroom

Nature Object: Wildflowers

In the fresh air with birds soaring high overhead, Jesus taught his famous "Sermon on the Mount." Looking into the anxious, care-worn faces of many in the crowd, He noted their burdens. He saw the eager countenances of the children and the care-lined faces of those with graying hair.

He proposed a simple cure. The precise prescription is recorded in Matthew 6:28: "Consider the lilies [wildflowers] of the field..." Jesus, as Creator, loves variety, having created over one million species of flowering plants. In the wonderworld of nature, flowers are fragrant reminders of the beauty that once graced planet earth.

Flowers have been called wanderers from Eden, still retaining their purity and beauty from a world that has been lost. Most wildflowers grow without any human thought of care or wisdom. None of these perfumed blossoms ever went to school. A close look reveals beauty, design, perfection, wisdom, and mystery.

Jesus said, "Consider...", look closely, ponder, commune with the "wildflowers of the field." Which one did Jesus specifically mean? I would like to suggest He might have plucked a dandelion in its mature gray-haired stage, blew away the seeds into the face of a little child looking up. In the following pages we will discover its secrets.

 PRACTICAL PROJECT

Go out into the countryside and see how many different varieties of wildflowers you can find. What do they all have in common: leaves, flowers, roots? We could actually write a book on any one of them and we would find they all teach lessons similar to the dandelion. Press the flowers and make notebooks, identifying each.

Outdoor Classroom

7

A Fragrance of Love

Nature Object: A Weed

The Dandelion is a common wayfaring flower that grows in yards, gardens, or fields. You may find them on mountain tops or valleys or along the side of the road. They grow on every continent and every island of the world. North America had seven native species of dandelions growing here until European settlers introduced four more. One of these new species from Europe is the focus of this book.

Because the supply exceeds the demand, dandelions have been considered by many people to be one of the most hated, poisoned, chopped, cut, rooted out, of all plants. Yet, in spite of man's attempts to exterminate, this flower continues to propagate and grow all over the countryside.

Jesus said, "And you will be hated by all for My name's sake. But he who endures to the end will be saved" (Matthew 10:22). Endurance is what Paul wrote about when he said love has no limit to its endurance, no end to its trust. Love never fades in its hope; it can outlast anything. It is in fact, the one thing that still stands when all else is gone. See 1 Corinthians 13:7.

In this book we shall consider how dandelions reveal 10 secrets of endurance. This flower grows and endures what would kill most flowers. It is living proof of the principle of the eight-beatitudes found in Matthew 5:10—to return good for evil as demonstration of mature love and self-control. This flower seems to say, "Go ahead, do your worst to me, while I do my best for you."

These yellow blossoms can be stepped on, dug up, chopped, yet it never attempts to slap or seek revenge, it just continues to grow and multiply. How does it endure such mistreatment and thrive? Consider how it grows.

PRACTICAL PROJECT

Take a dandelion plant and take a pair of scissors and cut off its blossom. Continue to cut off its blossom every time it grows and see how many times you can do this before it actually dies.

A Fragrance of Love

The Leaf of a Dandelion

Nature Object: Leaf

The notched dark green leaves hold the first secret of the dandelion's endurance. The deep notched tooth-like appearance of the leaf gives it the French name *dent de lion*, which means tooth of the lion. The scientific name for this plant is *Taraxacum officinale*. The green leaves growing just above the root, growing in a circle, shade out other plants, thus preserving nutrients and moisture for its own growth.

The dandelion's leaves exude an ethylene gas that discourages competition from other plants. In Luke 8:14, Jesus tells the parable of the sower, how thorns sucked up the moisture and thus there was never enough left to bring seeds to maturity. The dandelion's leaves resolve this problem by removing from its environment that which does not minister to its life.

Our time of life has only so many hours per day. We may become so preoccupied with sports, watching television, or playing computer games, that we are starved for want of the very best, which is Jesus. We can even be so busy with good things, like doing chores around the house and helping people, that we forget to feed our own souls. Satan invents unnumbered ways to occupy our minds so we may not dwell upon the great truth of our Savior's sacrifice. He knows that if he can divert our minds from Jesus, he has us caught.

Like the dandelion, we need to protect our environment with the atmosphere of Jesus, like the ethylene gas that would discourage competition of the devil's unnumbered schemes to sidetrack us into work or pleasures so we have no time for prayer, bible study, and to learn of Jesus. "If we endure, we shall also reign with Him. If we deny Him, He will also deny us. If we are faithless, He remains faithful; He cannot deny Himself" (2 Timothy 2:12,13). A godly "no," that is in harmony with the biblical "Thou shalt not," greatly simplifies the problems of life.

 ## PRACTICAL PROJECT

Carefully notice a few large dandelion plants and mark them. Under the leaves of one, carefully notice what grows there, if anything. Return each week to see if anything is growing or does it stay stunted? Try planting some radish seeds under the leaf of the dandelion, and see if any will sprout. Is there anything in our environment that will restrain our spiritual growth, such as too many hours of television, computer games, friends, or telephone calls? Is there anything we need to remove from our environment so that there will be sufficient time to grow in Jesus?

The Leaf of a Dandelion

A Daily Schedule

Nature Object: Bract and Blossom

The golden orb's second secret of endurance is a daily schedule. Each flower protects itself at night by a leaf shelter called bracts. This flower is one among many who open and close their flower petals on a daily basis. The dandelion takes one full hour to open its bracts and face a new day. After opening, with untiring perseverance it locks right in on the sun, like a radar screen its head will turn with the rotation of the sun across the sky absorbing its light and warmth. At twilight the bracts will take another hour to close up the work of the day and prepare for the night.

Do you take time when you wake up to talk to Jesus, to exchange your weakness for His strength, your ignorance for His wisdom, your frailty for His might? When the day is over do you take some time to thank Him for that day's fresh grace? Do you spend some time to clear your conscience to make sure you are at peace with God and man at the close of the day?

This lifestyle of the dandelion may be what Jesus had in mind when He said, "Therefore do not worry, saying 'What shall we eat?' or 'What shall we drink?' or 'What shall we wear?' For after all these things the Gentiles seek. For your heavenly Father knows that you need all these things. But seek first the kingdom of God and His righteousness, and all these things shall be added to you" (Matthew 6:31-33).

Like the dandelion, the prophet Daniel successfully merged two professions, prime minister of a pagan world government and a prophet for the living God. Three times a day he habitually went to a special place, knelt down, and prayed with thanksgiving. The power for his successful life came not from within but from above. Daniel, like the dandelion, made connecting with God his first and last work every day.

God's ways in nature are never hurried. The dandelion lives an unrushed day. It obeys the laws of nature perfectly. God will show his love and power in your life just as surely as in the dandelion's life, as you seek Him first.

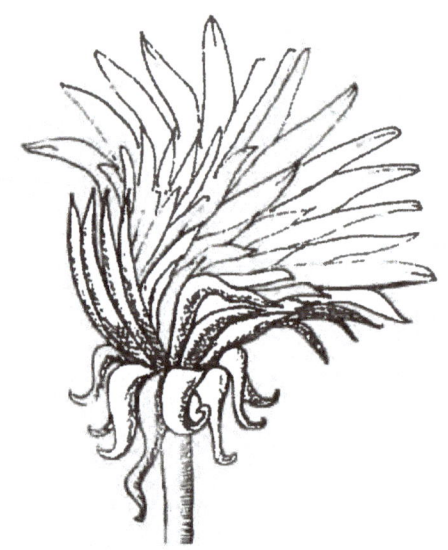

 ## PRACTICAL PROJECT

Find the length of time it takes for a dandelion blossom to open in the morning and how long it takes for the blossom to close at night. Apply these same principles to your life by spending time looking to Jesus every morning and every night. If it is warm enough outside, find a special place where you can talk with God and notice how His blessings change your day.

A Daily Schedule

Unity

Nature Object: Floret

The third secret of the dandelion's endurance is unity. The dandelion is a composite flower, which means that the flower is made up of many little flowers. They all live together, as it were, in one house, and each flower has a very large family of children.

Each yellow petal is called a floret, which means it is one complete flower capable of reproducing another complete dandelion plant. There can be 125 to 250 floret children in each flower house, depending on its size. All its children eat from a common yellow table, the stem. They all get their food from the pantry, the root. These floret children are squeezed tightly, as if snuggled in together. They live in very close harmony. You can put your ear down and listen. You will not hear them quarrel, grumble, or fight. They well illustrate the harmony God desires for our family.

These flower children do not run and play and sleep just anywhere they wish. If you look closely you will see three ways the dandelion florets operate in harmony and yet preserve their own individuality. 1) The florets limit their freedom so as not to take selfish advantage of the floret living right next door. 2) All the floret children share the special characteristic that makes them part of the dandelion family—they each experience the joy of service by giving freely of their special gifts and abilities to those who visit their home. 3) They bloom in the watch care and security of their heavenly Father. They explicitly obey the law and order that make this family function in perfect harmony. They illustrate how to "Be kindly affectionate to one another, in honor giving preference to one another" (Romans 12:10).

 ### PRACTICAL PROJECT

Pick two dandelion blossoms, one larger and one smaller. Count their petals. Are they both the same? Take a magnifying glass and see if you can identify all the specific parts that make up one floret flower child. How can your family care for each other in such a way that all may mature and use their unique talents and skills without grumbling or fighting?

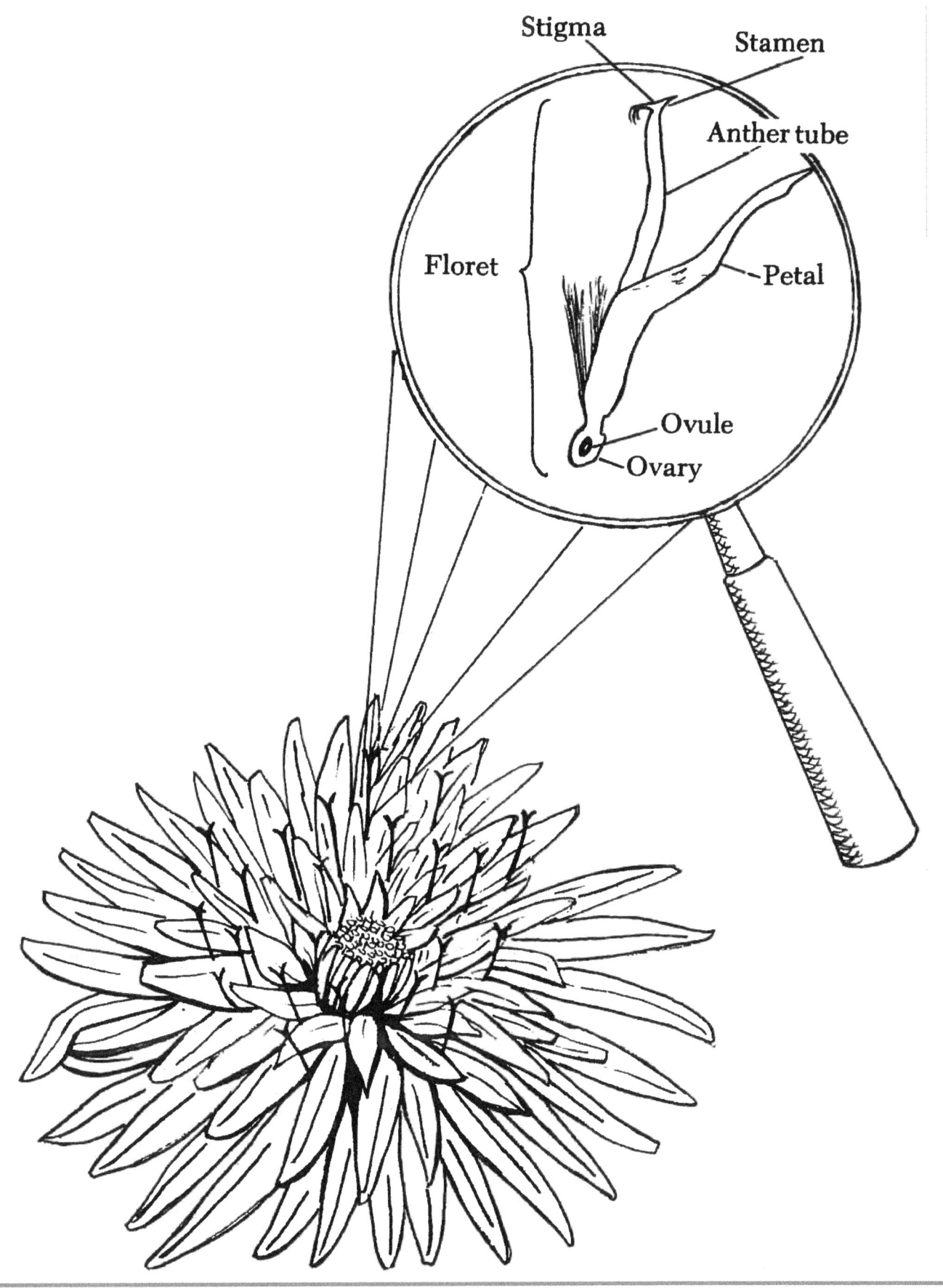

 # The Dandelion's Root System

Nature Object: Root

The fourth secret of the dandelion's endurance is its root system. This is the way it receives and stores energy. As the dandelion strives for greater growth, the carrot-like root seeks moisture. A large dandelion may have a tap root that reaches three feet in length. In fact the tap root keeps growing longer year after year.

This plant receives energy and vitality from the sun, rain, air, and soil. It not only uses this for day to day growth, but it also stores some of it for hard times in its tuber root.

Likewise, the Christian delights in scriptures for day-to-day growth. He memorizes and meditates on God's Word. The verses may be stored in our mind for future use. "Your word have I hidden in my heart" (Psalm 119:11).

Any piece of the dandelion's root, if left in the ground, will grow a new plant. This is one of the reasons why this plant survives.

We may build our lives rooted on human thinking, or upon God's unshakable eternal word. Note the following promise: "To be strengthened with power through His Spirit in the inner man; that Christ may dwell in your hearts through faith; and that you being rooted and grounded in love, may be able to comprehend with all the saints what is the width and length and height and depth—to know the love of Christ which passes knowledge, that you may be filled with all the fullness of God" (Ephesians 3:16–19). How long are our roots?

To store or save scripture in the memory is one way to be "rooted and grounded" in Christ. When was the last time you committed a portion of scripture to memory?

 ### PRACTICAL PROJECT

Dig up a root of a large dandelion plant. How long is it? Our sin nature has deep roots that go all the way back to Adam. Take the root, chop it up, dry it, then use it to make a tea.

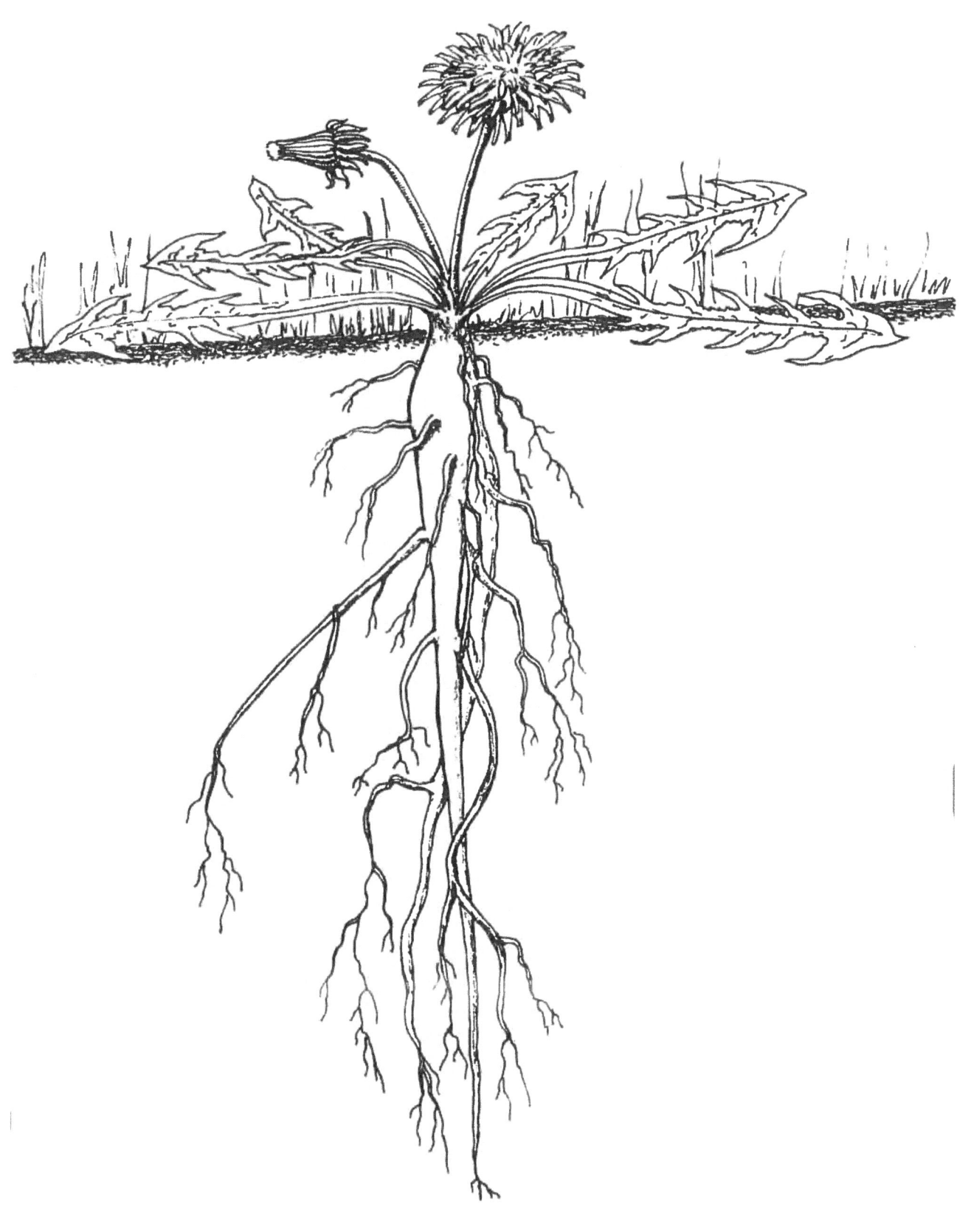

The Dandelion's Root System

The Stem

Nature Object: Stem and Osmosis

The fifth secret of endurance is the stem. The stem holds the flower vertically while delivering food and energy. The stem is that hollow straw that children love to play with. Why is it hollow? In the thin walls of this green tube, many wonderful processes are functioning to cause nature's silent pump to pull nutrition from the roots up to the flower.

Osmosis is the passage of water through a membrane usually at the root, from an area of higher concentration to an area of lower concentration. The membrane, or the outer surface of the root hair, chooses what comes in and what does not come in—the movement of molecules from a greater concentration to a lesser concentration. As the water and nutrients diffuse their way through the root, it enters the xylem tubes, which is called the sap stream. Just how this sap moves upward against the law of gravity, all the way to the flower head is still not clearly understood.

Fluid enters very tiny tubes called xylem cells. Because water has cohesion—the force that holds the water particles together—and adhesion—the force that causes water to stick to the walls of narrow tubes—all of this works together. Some believe that as the water is evaporated through blossom petals, those tiny cells, having given up their water, have created a tiny pull, which tends to pull the water up the stem. There appears to be no moving parts and the whole pump operation is entirely silent.

In a similar way, our weak selfish hearts receive Christ's love via the Holy Spirit. Operating similar to osmosis, heaven's strength will silently flow into our human weakness. In this way His strength will enter into every part of our sin weary lives, the stronger flowing into the weaker. This process is a beautiful description of one simple statement, "Do not be overcome by evil but overcome evil with good" (Romans 12:21). This is the foundation of the redemption plan.

On the center side of the hollow straw are xylem cells carrying fluids up to the blossom. On the outside of the stem are phloem cells carrying by products back down to the root. The Holy Spirit takes our prayers upward to heaven. (See Hebrews 4:14, 16; 10:11–28.) The Holy Spirit also brings divine power from heaven back down to us. (See John 15:2–6; 16:7–16). In this way we exchange selfishness for Christ's righteousness. We cooperate with the Holy Spirit by talking to God in prayer and receiving His word.

The stem serves another purpose: when the flower is mature and ready to send out its seed missionaries, the stem will stiffen, become strait and tall so the wind can catch the white silk and send the seeds on their airborne journey. We likewise, when prompted by the spirit can stand straight and tall, for we have something to tell of what God has done for us.

PRACTICAL PROJECT

Pick a dandelion blossom with its stem and place it in water with red or green cake coloring added. See if the stem will pull the color up into the blossom.

Try taking a stem and sucking some cool water up through the stem. Can you suck through it? How many things can be made from a stem?

The Stem

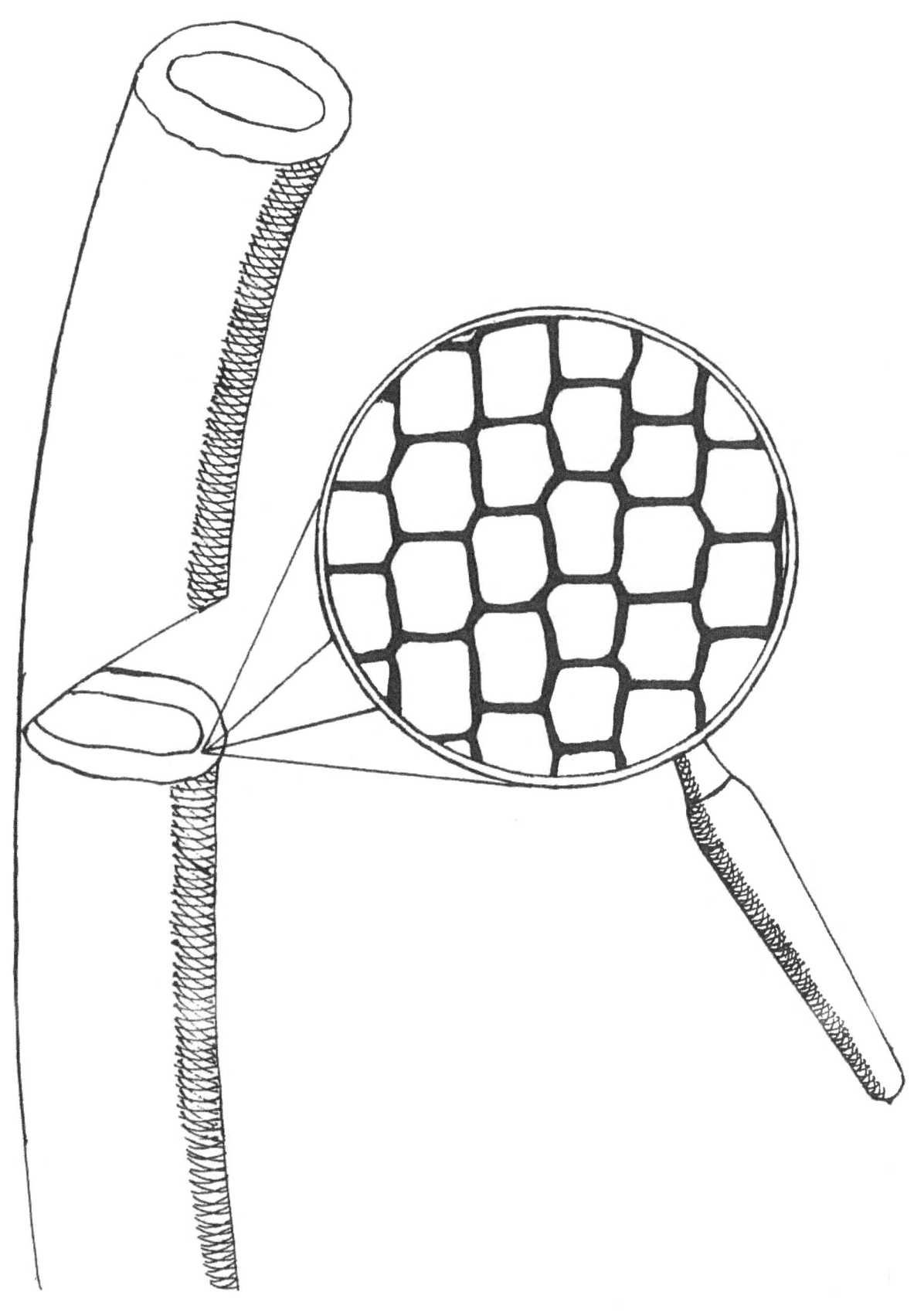

Flexibility

Nature Object: Growth Style

The sixth secret of endurance is flexibility. God's wisdom manifested in this stem seems almost unbelievable. I observed a dandelion growing in the middle of a creeping juniper bush in an effort to reach the sun. The stem grew almost two feet in length. However, this growth is flexible and that is the sixth secret of the dandelion's endurance—flexibility. It adjusts its growth according to the changing environment where it finds itself.

Dandelions, when mown where they are mown regularly, in our front yard, will grow their leaves absolutely flat and the dandelion blossoms will grow almost below the surface of the ground, same plant, same stem, yet it grows differently according to its environment.

Every flower that opens its petal to the sunshine, obeys the same great laws that guides the stars. How simple and beautiful and sweet its life. And yet one little flower finding itself in difficulties still keeps its same identity, principles, and purposes.

We don't seem to reason from cause to effect. We go over the same ground again and again until we learn life's greatest lesson: a complete distrust of self and an unshakable trust in God—in His word and His ways. When we learn this lesson the Holy Spirit can open our eyes to value reproof so we learn from our mistakes. "A prudent man foresees evil and hides himself. The simple pass on and are punished" (Proverbs 27:12).

A fool is one who never learns from his mistakes. He blames others or circumstances for his misuse or abuse of freedom or trust. "He who reproves a scoffer gets shame for himself and he who rebukes a wicked man gets himself a blemish. Do not reprove a scoffer lest he hate you. Rebuke a wise man and he will love you. Give instruction to a wise man and he will be still wiser. Teach a just man and he will increase in learning" (Proverbs 9:7–9).

 PRACTICAL PROJECT

Try running a lawn mower over a dandelion plant and watch what happens. Keep running it over the top and watch what happens to the leaves. See if you can find some long-stemmed ones that are growing in the shade. How long did the stems grow?

Unrelenting Effort

Nature Object: Early Spring Flower

The dandelion's seventh secret of endurance is its untiring effort. This flower is not lazy. It does not sleep away the morning hours. In fact, it is one of the very first flowers to blossom in the spring time. Sometimes you can even find it blooming with snow around it in the northern climates. In this way the dandelion gets a head start on other plants. In warmer climates the dandelion can bloom every month of the year, but in the northern climates they bloom especially in the early spring.

Some so called Christians do their sharing only at church or for those who they think good enough. Some share only one day a week, like only on Sabbath. Jesus however thought to apply the gospel to every person he met under every circumstance. He sees what fallen human nature can be when connected with him. When we feel worthless, Jesus sees our value. All summer long, through heat, dust, mud, or drought, the dandelion continues its daily growth. As the days get longer, the need for food and energy becomes more intense. Untiring effort is the basis of all endurance.

"Preach the word! Be ready in season and out of season. Convince, rebuke, exhort with all longsuffering and teaching. For the time will come when they will not endure sound doctrine, but according to their own desires, because they have itching ears, they heap up for themselves teachers" (2 Timothy 4:2–3).

Growth means change and change takes effort and requires energy. Through all the summer months the dandelion works. Only when the snow comes does it take a winter's nap.

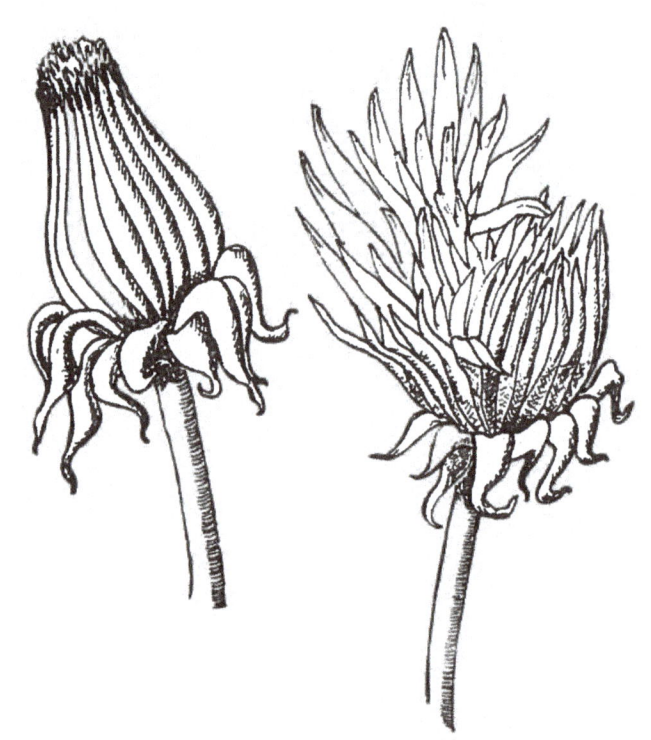

 PRACTICAL PROJECT

When spring comes, carefully notice when the first dandelion plant becomes visible. Count the days from when the green leaves appear till the yellow flower appears. Carefully note when it quits blooming. Measure its growth weekly. Are there times in the year when it grows more rapidly or more slowly?

Unrelenting Effort

23

Magnified Beauty

Nature Object: Stamen

"Consider the wildflowers of the field..." The word 'consider' means to 'look closely.' With a simple microscope, even at twenty power, we can view the tiny stamen. Similar to a ram's horn, it comes close to the very beginning of mystery of life. Behold, what internal hidden beauty. The stamen are covered with glass-like pointed spires covered with a living gold. On the point of these glass like needles the mysterious pollen is born.

Evolutionary theory says all things evolve from some need. Here we behold beauty that goes way beyond mere need. God is not content to provide that which would maintain mere existence. In the loveliness of the things of nature we can learn more of the wisdom of God than preachers know. The dandelion could have all that is needed for existence without this unseen beauty.

God has filled earth, air, and sky with glimpses of beauty to tell you of His loving thought for you. If He has flooded such infinite skill upon the things of nature for your happiness and joy, can you doubt that He will give you every needed blessing?

Satan delights in the dirty and the ugly. On the TV screen he makes ugliness appear beautiful. Imaginary monsters are made the hero. Useful toys are transformed into robots of destruction. What a contrast to the natural beauty of the things God has made. "He has made everything beautiful in its time" (Ecclesiastes 3:11).

 PRACTICAL PROJECT

Observe a dandelion plant and watch it go from bud to white fuzz. Carefully notice when the yellow flower opens. Are the stamen visible? Buy a cheap magnifying glass and look at the tiny stamens. When is the first day they appear curled? Is the pollen available on the first day that the bud opens? When does the pollen become visible? What part of the stamen produces the pollen? The glass spires or somewhere else? Consider, look closely!

Magnified Beauty

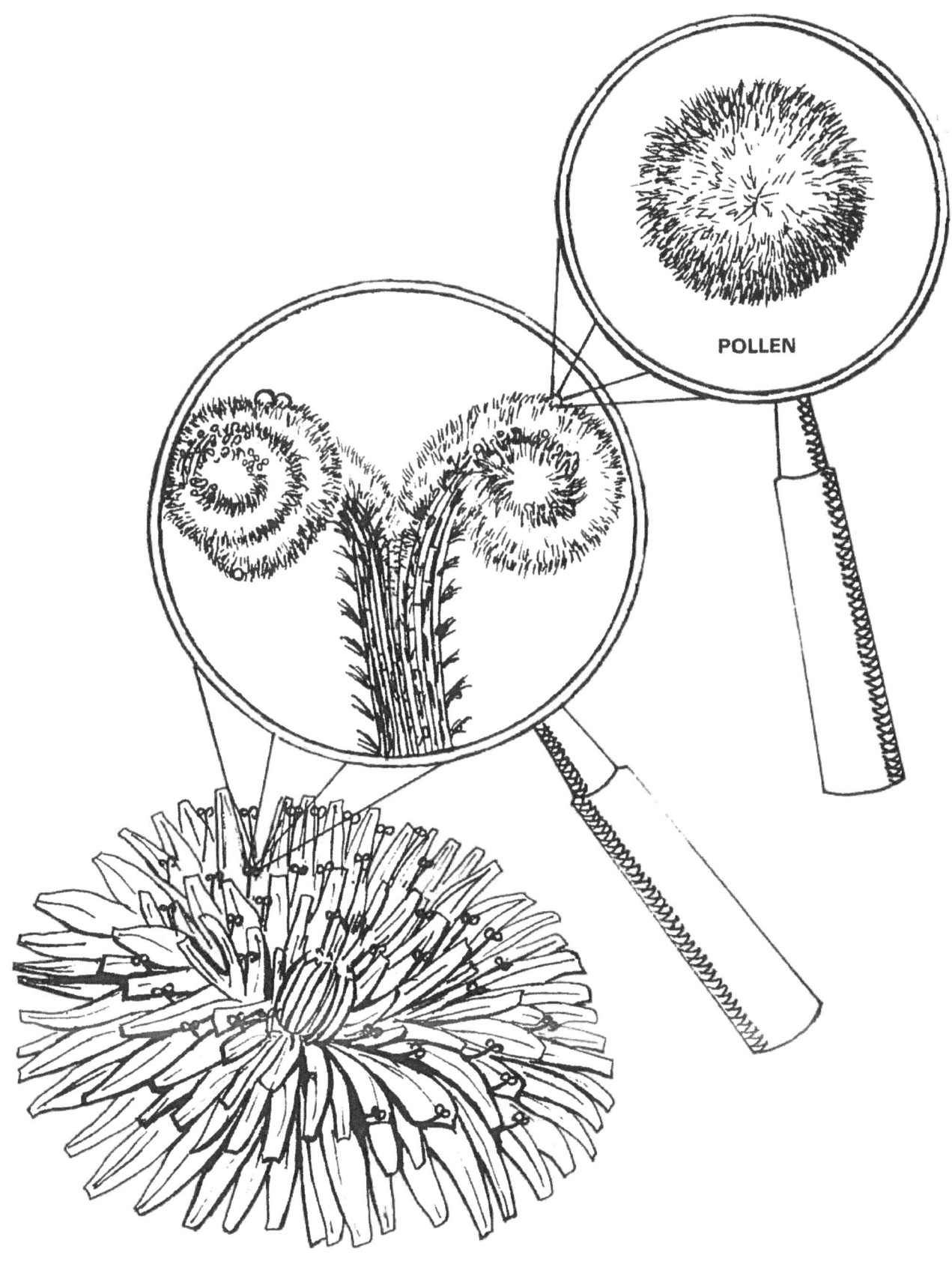

25

Character Beauty

Nature Object: Pollen

Consider! At every increase of magnification four things may be seen: Order; Design; Individuality; and Beauty.

Order is obedience to law. Some today would have us think there are no absolutes of right or wrong. If this kind of thinking were demonstrated in the pollen dust, what a mess and chaos we would see. Under a microscope we see the same order in every speck. Not chaos or muddle, but precise order. Design is the way a thing is shaped or arranged. Here is seen genius that only the Creator could conceive. The design follows consistent principles, yet no two grains of pollen are just exactly alike.

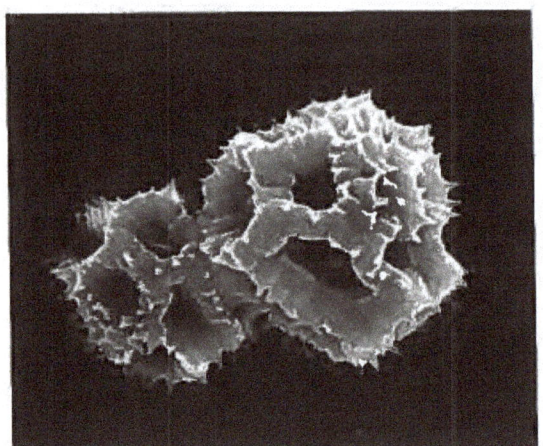

Individuality is seen with a harmonious pattern. The natural world tells us our Creator does not mass produce anything, not even pollen dust on a dandelion. Centuries ago God gave mankind 10 principles to live by. Only within the freedom of these principles can your value and worth be protected. James 1:25 calls these the perfect law of liberty. They are the 10 Commandments of Exodus 20.

From microscopic pollen we observe order, design, and individuality. Together they all make beauty.

If man could see small enough, even on the pollen, we would discover the energy of the atom itself. An Atom is made up of a nucleus around which spin particles called electrons, circling in their own law-abiding way. The whole world of physics and science rests on God's unchanging consistent order which is the same yesterday, today, and forever.

 PRACTICAL PROJECT

With paper and pencil try and draw a tree or leafy branch. How are the four qualities: order, design, beauty, and individuality revealed in what you see? Note the way pine needles are arranged on its twigs. Then take a look at your bedroom, dresser drawers, your desk, and the bathroom. Can we still see heaven's order?

Character Beauty

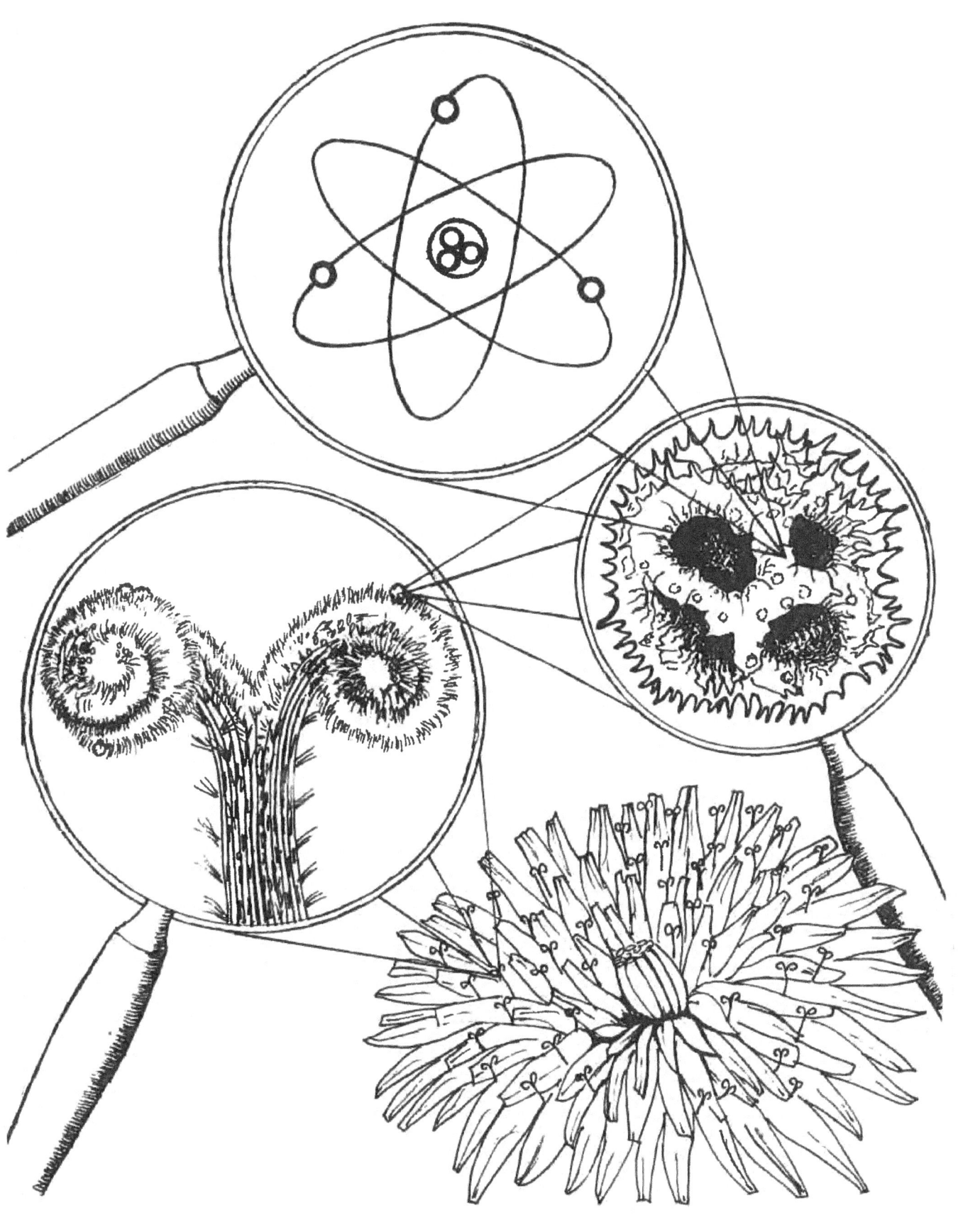

Hidden Beauty

Nature Object: Pollen Magnified

The pollen dust in this picture is magnified 5,2000 times. Looking very closely through the electron microscope we can see its hidden beauty. The electron microscope magnifies with exceeding great power. If we want to look at a piece of matter one cubic centimeter in size, the electron microscope can enlarge it so much that it would take seven years of continuous eight hour days just to photograph it.

We see these fragile golden ornaments that grace the dandelion stamen. The smaller pictures are magnified 640 times. Notice carefully how pollen always has six ray-like fingers that surround its golden dust. Absolutes are followed in God's natural world. They obey the Creator's laws consistently. "Let all things be done decently and in order" (1 Corinthians 14:40).

With this special instrument, the human eye can see what otherwise would be invisible. Jesus is more concerned with beautiful thoughts on the inside than mere outward looks. "The Lord does not see as man sees; for man looks at the outward appearance, but the Lord looks at the heart" (1 Samuel 16:7).

We need to learn to see life from God's point of view, from the spiritual perspective, from what scripture calls the inner man. We may be tempted to rely on outward adorning for lack of inner character beauty. "Do not let your beauty be the outward adorning, of the arranging of the hair, or in gold, or of putting on fine pearls; but let it be the hidden person of the heart, with the incorruptible ornament of a gentle and quiet spirit, which is very precious in the sight of God" (1 Peter 3:3,4).

Dandelion pollen shows our Creator is a perfect workman. He makes hidden beauty just as carefully as He makes the visible beauty. God is a lover of true genuine beauty.

PRACTICAL PROJECT

Try getting a surplus microscope from a local high school or college. Shake some pollen dust on the glass slide and take a look, increasing the power. Start with low power then increase to a higher power. Compare dandelion pollen to the pollen of other wildflowers. How do the different kinds of pollen vary from each other?

Bees take pollen to make honey. How can they take these little structures and reprocess them into something sweet? Try tasting pollen with your tongue. How does it taste? Study this micrograph of dandelion pollen and ask yourself, why the pointed barbicels? What are the little holes about? Why does it have six rays around the circle? How does the stamen know how to manufacture this little bit of pollen? What does pollen do for the plant? As a family study 1 Corinthians 14:40.

Hidden Beauty

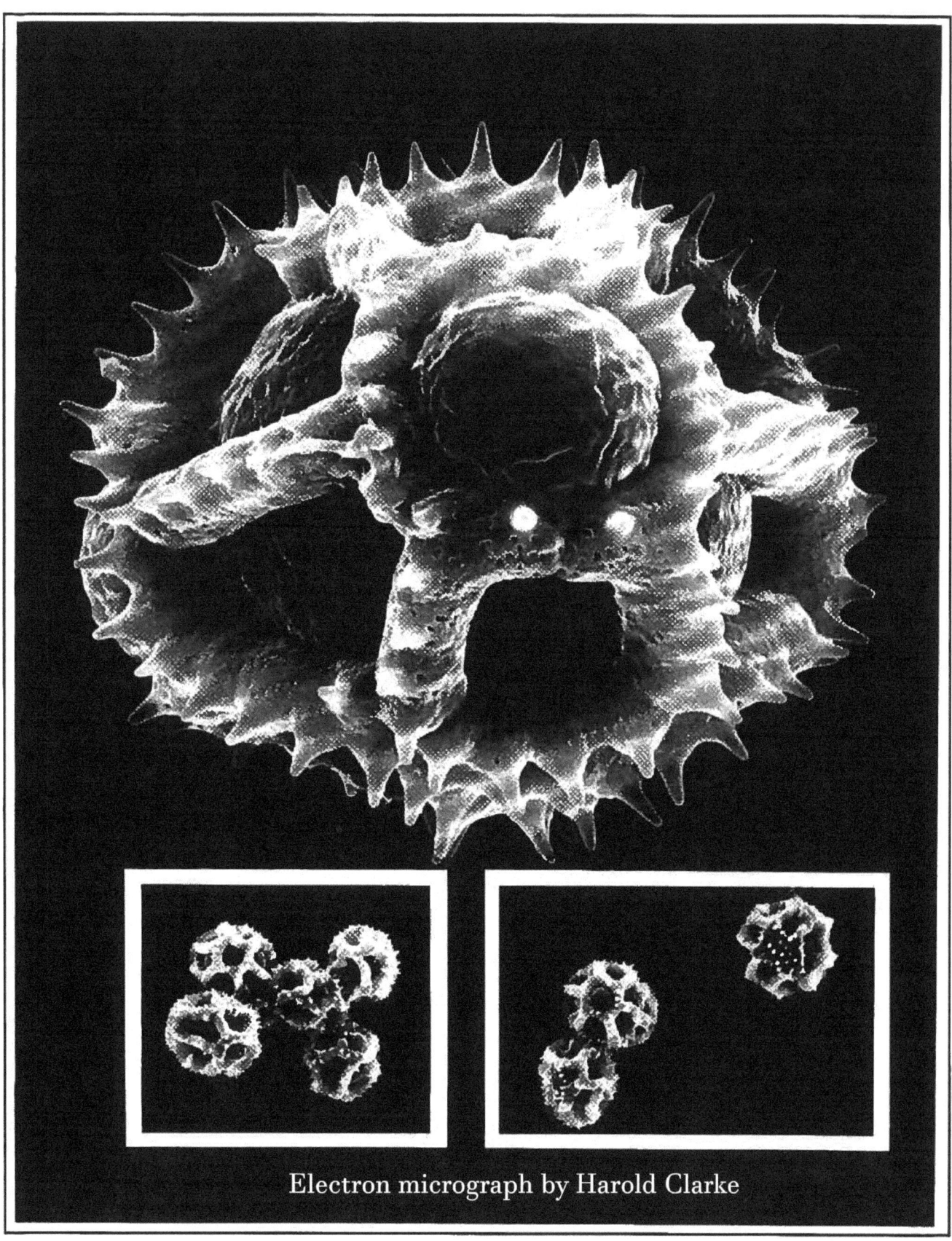

Electron micrograph by Harold Clarke

The Dormant Stage
Nature Object: Enclosed by Bract

Dandelion blossoms normally open about the time you go to school and close about the time you return. This continues on a daily basis until the seeds are fertilized. After the seeds are fertilized with pollen the flower appears to dry up and die. The old bract, the wall-like structure, encloses the flower for a period of one to two weeks. This looks like the death or end of the flower. This is similar to losing a friend. At school we have a desire to be accepted by our friends. One day they may ask you to break a school rule or disobey your parents. You refuse and they laugh. This is not pleasant and it appears for a time you have lost your friends. But when you stand alone for right there is a friend who stays beside you—Jesus. He knows what it is like to walk alone and be laughed at.

While hidden from view by the bract's protection, the dandelion seeds ripen to maturity. The silks grow taller and lighter. In a similar way, it appears no one will be your friend. However, character is developing for you on the inside. "But there is a friend who sticks closer than a brother" (Proverbs 18:24). Steadfastness to right for a time may cost you the loss of false friends. But later you will find true friends with similar qualities and together you will reveal to the world God's beauty of truth and right.

At the end of a one to two-week period the bract protection opens. When it opens we see silky little parachutes ready to carry the seeds away.

Seeds ride on the air currents. Then they fall to the ground and appear to be dead. Months later a new plant sprouts up and the dandelion once again begins its story of life.

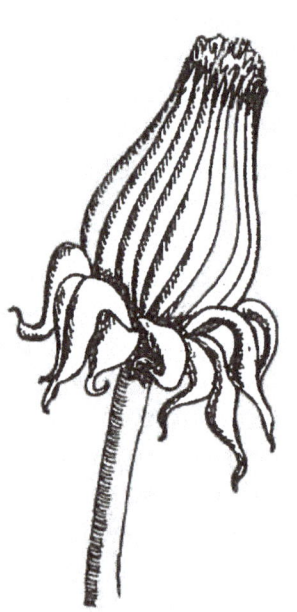

 PRACTICAL PROJECT

Find a dandelion plant going into the dormant stage. Mark the length of time it remains closed. This dormant stage could be like a period of time we choose to be alone with God, that scripture might be more deeply hidden by the Holy Spirit in our heart and mind. Have you had any dormant stages in your life where you are still and quiet for an extended period of time for the purpose of growing in knowing God?

The Dormant Stage

Spreading Seeds

Nature Object: Seed with Silk

The eighth secret of endurance is the way it spreads it seed. Every part of the dandelion plant works toward one common goal, reproducing itself by way of seeds. Wind is the basic means the dandelion uses to give its seeds away. The purpose of the seed is to produce new plants. The seed has a special parachute attached to the top of itself called the pappus.

Each part of the dandelion flower works toward one common goal—to spread seeds and reproduce itself. At the white-head stage of the dandelion's life, the seeds are attached to a special parachute called the pappus. A careful study of this silk seed-carrying apparatus is truly amazing. The plant relies upon the wind as the basic means of transportation to carry its seeds away. The force of the wind determines how far the seeds will go. Another factor is the humidity of the air. The pressured silk will stay aloft as long as the humidity is less than 70%. But then the humidity gets higher than 70% (like just before it rains), then the silk parachute will fold up and the seed will drop to the ground. Then if it rains it gets pounded into the ground. All this works together, not as a handy accident, but rather as the planning of a Divine mind.

The wind determines the distance the seed will go before the humidity causes it to drop. "The wind blows where it wishes, you hear the sound of it, but cannot tell where it comes from or where it goes. So is everyone that is born of the spirit" (John 3:8).

The basic purpose of the Holy Spirit is witness, "But you shall receive power when the Holy Spirit has come upon you and you shall be witnesses to me in Jerusalem and in Judea and in Samaria, and to the end of the earth" (Acts 1:8).

Your witness tells what you have seen and experienced. The dandelion never tries to be a rose or a tulip, never tries to be an oak tree, just a dandelion. But what a marvelous story it has to tell. It keeps telling the same story over and over again. The dandelion starts sharing wherever its seed is put down. It never tires of telling the old story of what God's creative power and wisdom has done for it.

 PRACTICAL PROJECT

On a bright sunny day take some of the white headed pappus dandelion seeds inside the house and then turn on the shower. Set these seeds in a pan nearby and see if you have a humidity measuring device. Watch the humidity go up and then watch the parachutes close up. How do these parachutes know when the humidity reaches a certain level that it is time to close up? Isn't that a nice arrangement just before it rains, so the seed can go back down to the ground?

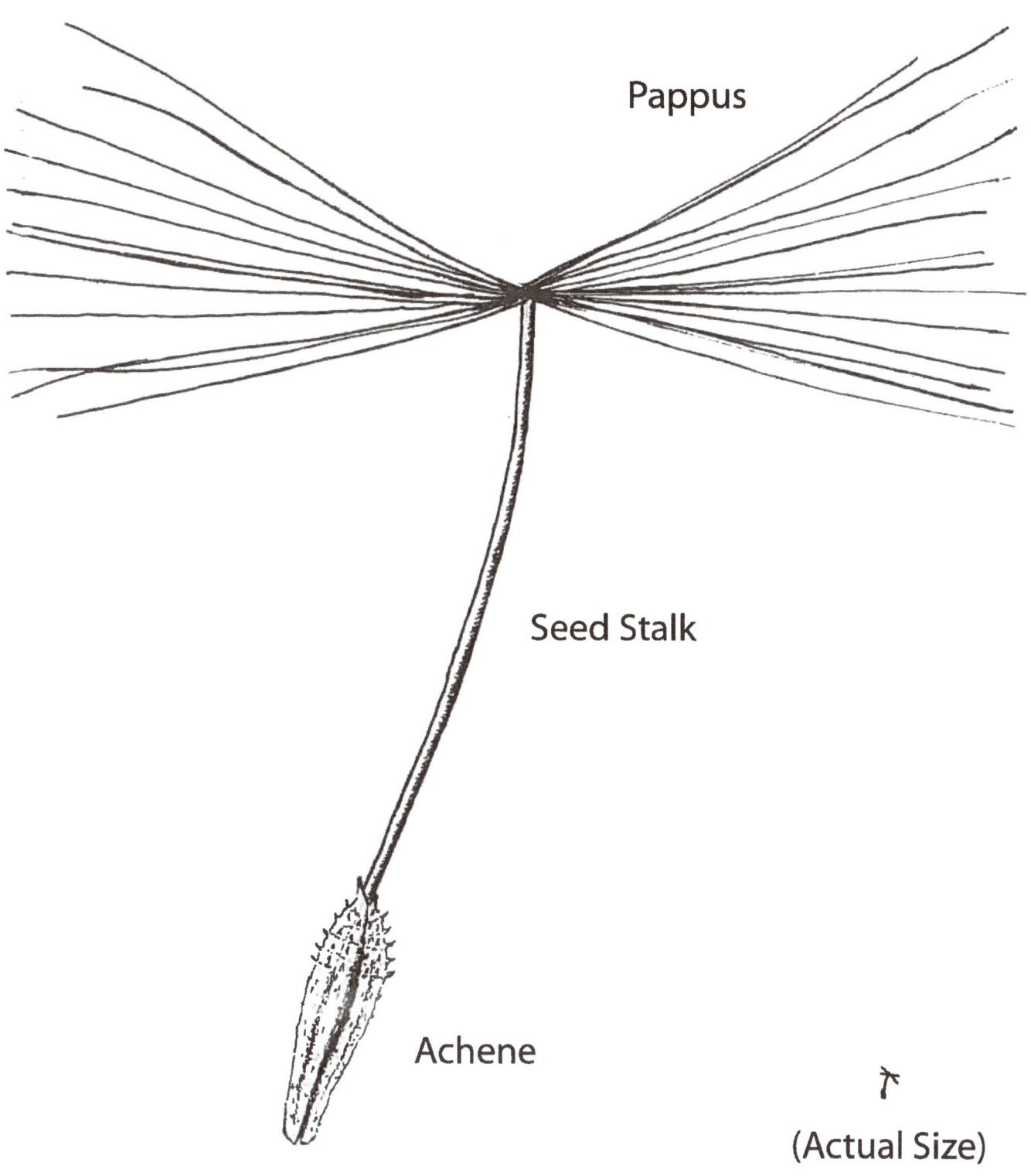

Seed Determines the Harvest

Nature Object: Brown Seed

Brown tough and horny, this seed is not attractive but it is effective in starting the life of another dandelion plant. The seed is about the size of a grain of rice. Locked inside that little capsule is the sleeping life of another dandelion. These seeds may be dropped in the briny ocean and soaked for up to 28 days and if carried ashore they will still germinate and grow.

Experts tell us in the open field we may find as many as 100,000 dormant seeds of various kinds, per square yard. These seeds are waiting patiently for the right conditions that may cause them to spring into life. Dandelion seeds can easily lay dormant for 30 or 40 years before springing into life. Dandelion seeds always produce dandelions. God made a law that everything will produce after its kind (see Genesis 1:11, 12). This means dandelions will never become tulips, roses, or daises, just dandelions.

"Do not be deceived, God is not mocked; for whatever a man sows, that he will also reap. For he who sows to his flesh will of the flesh reap corruption, but he who sows to the Spirit will of the Spirit reap everlasting life. And let us not grow weary while doing good, for in due season we shall reap if we do not lose heart" (Galatians 6:7–9).

Seeds illustrate the power of His words planted in the soil of our human heart. The Bible is His divine seed catalog. Each promise is precious and will reproduce the life of its Author, Jesus. Christian youth may deny Jesus by dirty jokes and swearing, but youth with the seed of Jesus in their heart can say, "I have committed my life to Christ, I cannot enjoy this." They can perseveringly and decisively walk away with Jesus in their heart. His seed endures and will bloom at the right time. Jesus said He is coming again to harvest the good seed. See Matthew 13:37–43. Jesus will return to harvest His seed as surely as dandelion seeds continue to grow new dandelion plants.

FAMILY PROJECT

Try planting some dandelion seeds in a flowerpot. Water them and put them in the sunlight. Carefully note how long it takes the seeds to sprout a new dandelion plant.

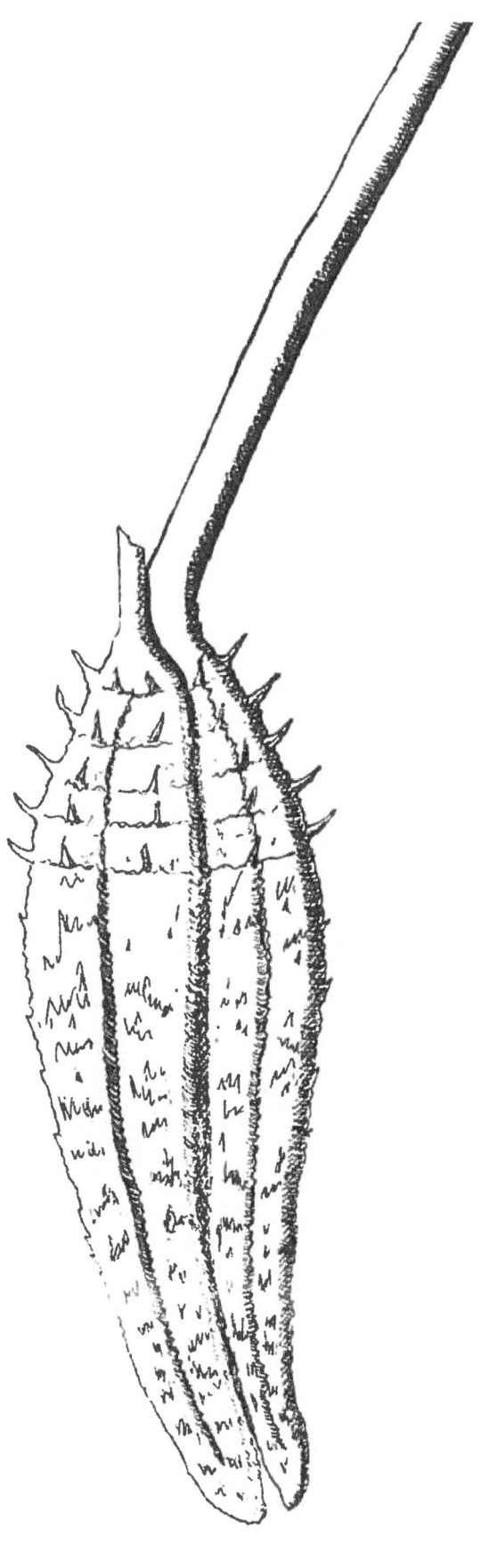

Hidden Hooks

Nature Object: Silk

Nature has many surprises for the careful observer. Consider the soft silk of the dandelion pappus. Under the microscope, multiplied around 600 times, we can see the soft silk is more like barbed wire. The streamers of the pappus are covered with tiny barb-like briars similar to briars on a blackberry bush. The dandelion seems to have many secret little hooks.

These hidden hooks are like our motives. Motives are why one does what one does. Motives may be of two kinds, selfish or unselfish. Only Christ's pure motives can overpower our selfish one. This secret motive will be made visible in the judgment. Then the judgment microscope will be looking at our life's record, examining every motive. Soon our life will pass the scrutiny of the great white throne of judgment, "for God will bring every work into judgment, whether it is good or whether it is evil" (Ecclesiastes 12:14).

As we look at each other we cannot discern the hidden motives of the heart. We can't see the hidden hooks and we sometimes judge unwisely. We approve or condemn other youth by their actions. Many actions we approve, God may condemn, and some we condemn, God may approve. Why? Because our natural eyes see only the silky exterior but God sees the hidden hooks of motive.

Are my words and actions done to the glory of God and to bless my playmates? Or are they to the advantage and glory of me? No other question will be necessary. Motive reveals all hidden hooks under the heavenly judgment microscope.

 ## PRACTICAL PROJECT

With a small magnifying glass look around the yard at different plants and weeds and see how many hidden hooks are found on other plants.

The "silk" part of the dandelion can also tell the relative humidity of the air. The white "silk" will close up when the humidity gets above 70%. On a hot clear day place a drop of water on the silk part and see what happens. Why do you think God arranged the silk to open and close in this way? How does the silk part help the dandelion spread its seed?

Hidden Hooks

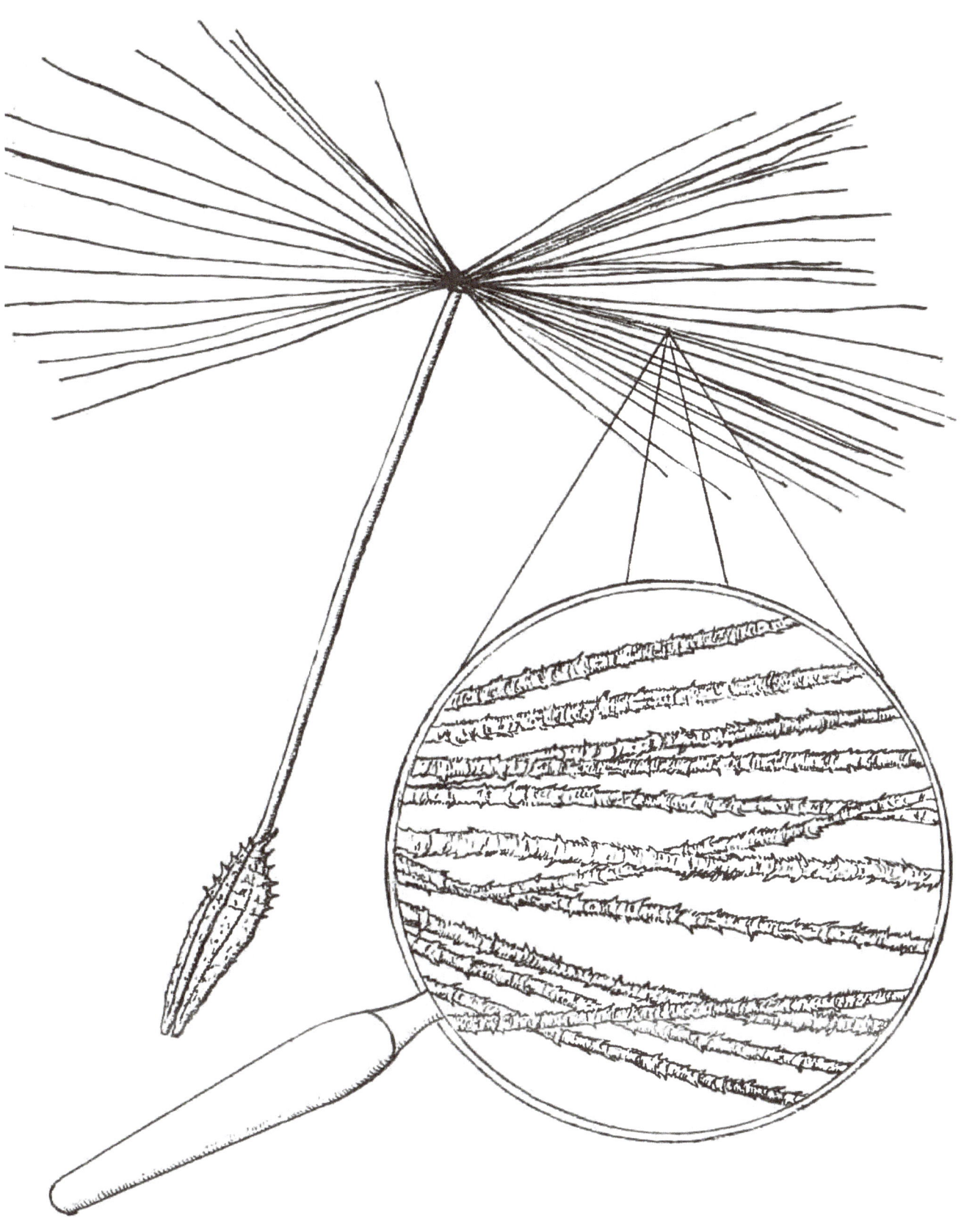

The Cross

Nature Object: Seeds Gone

At maturity this flower gives away everything it has ever lived for, namely its seed children. It keeps none for itself. As a result, dandelions continue to grow. Should the dandelion become selfish and keep all its seeds dandelions would cease to be. This is the ninth secret of the dandelion's endurance. It lives and practices self-denial.

Jesus illustrated this principle of self-denial at the cross of Calvary (See 2 Corinthians 8:9). Jesus was more than a martyr dying for a great cause. He was the Creator demonstrating His great love for us by His ultimate self-denial and laying down His life for His creatures for an insecure planet, Earth.

Jesus's self-denial was made visible to us when He was "made in the likeness of sinful flesh" (Romans 8:3). As a man He became what John the Baptist called, "The Lamb of God who takes away the sins of the world" (John 1:29). When Jesus died, inanimate nature sympathized with its Author. The sun refused to shine for six hours. There was a great earthquake, graves were split open, dead bodies were cast out. A mysterious darkness surrounded His cross like a dark funeral shroud.

As the dandelion gives its seeds away that another generation of dandelions may live, so Jesus yielded His life for those He loved, that a whole generation, yea a whole world of sinners, might live. "He saved others, but Himself He could not save," His enemies said, and they spoke the truth (Matthew 27:42). Jesus could not save His life at the cross and still pay our penalty for sin, which was death. Paul put it well when he said in 1 Corinthians 1:18, "For the message of the cross is foolishness to those who are perishing, but to us that are being saved, it is the power of God."

 PRACTICAL PROJECT

Watch a dandelion silk as the winds blow away the seeds. What happens to the stem? Carefully check your dandelion plant daily to see what happens to that stem—a left over part of the cross, if you please. How long is it before the dandelion plants produce a new yellow head? You might carefully note the number of days from bud to when flower seeds are passed on and there are no more remnants of its cross left behind. How many times does one dandelion plant do this in one season?

The Cross

Service and Ministry

Nature Object: Insects on Blossom

Not only do dandelions give their seeds away, they also give their pollen away. The tenth secret of our yellow wayfaring flower is that of service and ministry.

Bees love to receive pollen from the dandelion and this blossom is valuable in the production of golden honey. The ant also is a frequent guest at this yellow table. Pheasants, grouse, and other birds favor the seeds. The leaves are relished by deer. Dandelion leaves are high in vitamins A, B, calcium, phosphorous, and iron. Young leaves in the spring make a delicious tossed salad, or cooked as spinach. Every part of the dandelion flower is actually edible by man.

People from the island of Minorca, one of the islands of the Balearic Sea east of Spain, avoided starvation by eating dandelion roots when locust had devoured all their plants. These roots may be sliced and boiled in salt water and served like potatoes. It is estimated that there are 10 million insects along with 2 million spiders per grassy acre. Many dine frequently at the dandelion house.

What do visitors see in your house? What do you offer your friends when they come to visit? Are your toys and treasures full of lasting golden value? Are your games uplifting and worthwhile, or perhaps foolish or even harmful? Isaiah 39:4 asks the question, "What have they seen in your house?"

What do you contribute to your family's lifestyle? Do you have to be told what to do when you know it needs doing? Do you shirk your job? Do you work cheerfully and willingly? If you would be great in God's kingdom, then we must learn the lesson of the dandelion, to be a servant to all. See Mark 10:42–45.

PRACTICAL PROJECT

Spend some time carefully watching a dandelion flower. How many insects come to dine at its flower table in one hour? You might even try watching for several hours. Look very carefully because some insects that live and dine there are very small.

Counterfeits

Nature Object: Similar Blossom

At a quick glance, the flower on the opposite page looks like a dandelion. But in reality, this perennial flower has the scientific name Sonchus arvensis. Counterfeits are found even in the world of flowers and often go undetected by the hasty observer. Jesus said, "Consider," look closely at the flowers of the field. Learn to heart-read her messages. Today we live a fast pace. Satan is a fast operator who passes things before us quickly so we can't examine his fraud. He mixes truth with error till it seems like we know nothing for sure.

With a quick look the sow thistle and the dandelion appear similar. Youth are urged to live life quickly, before it is over. Yet, God offers us life without end. Music pounds out its message before we have time to examine its value or where it ends. Foods are gulped between appointments without a thought of nutrition or value. Television grabs our eyes and scene after scene flashes through our imagination before we can decide whether it is right or wrong. Drugs offer a quick trip before you know its destination. Our generation has been called the throw-away generation. Nothing seems to have lasting value. The Bible calls it the last generation. It will end.

Counterfeits are always of less value than the real. The sow thistle is not of the same value as the real dandelion. Likewise, quick friends and quick pleasures are quickly gone and we are left cheated. "Trust in the Lord with all your heart, and lean not to your own understanding; in all your ways acknowledge Him, and He shall direct your paths" (Proverbs 3:5, 6).

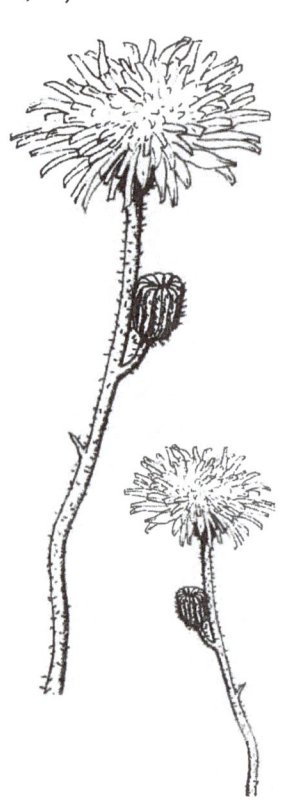

 PRACTICAL PROJECT

On a walk with the family, see how many flowers you find that have counterfeits besides just dandelions. If you are weeding the garden, carefully notice the plants you are cultivating and the weeds that attempt to grow beside it. Some weeds when they are young, look very much like the plant you are trying to cultivate. When they grow awhile it becomes obvious which they really are.

Counterfeits

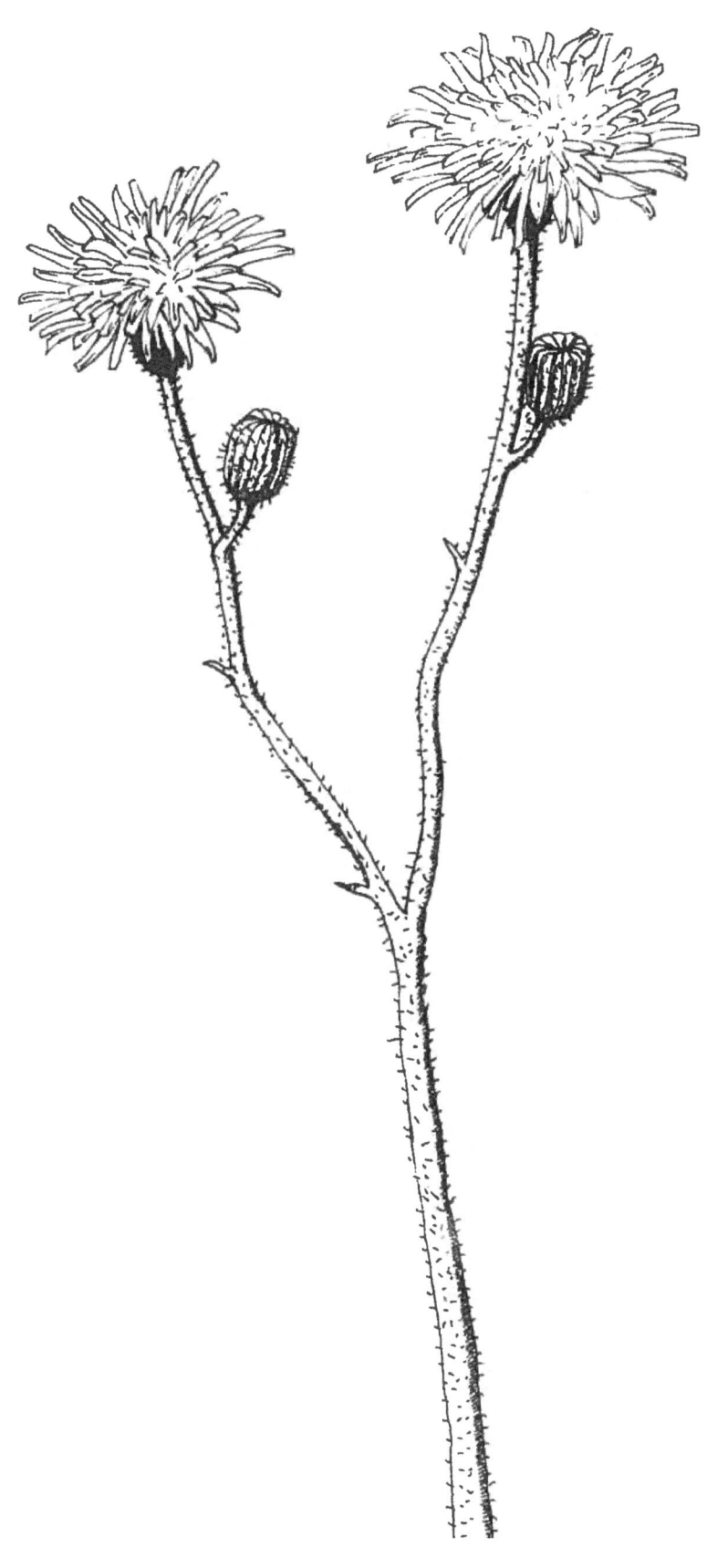

Detecting a Counterfeit

Nature Object: Compared Blossom

We can identify the real dandelion from a flower that looks similar by testing the qualities. First, there must be an absolute standard of the real flower's qualities. Second, we must compare the flowers in question to that absolute standard. Do this for the flowers on the facing page.

	REAL	**COUNTERFEIT**
1. Leaves	Dark green, smooth, deep-notched, grows in a circle	Green, hairy, unnotched, grows in a circle
2. Stem	Smooth, round, hollow in the middle, with one yellow flower on the top	Thorn-like, hairy, round stem, more than one yellow flower on the top
3. Roots	A tuber tap root, grows deep	Short tap root
4. Bracts	Has a skirt on the bracts	Has no skirt
5. Conclusion	Taraxacum officinale	Sonchus arvensis

Truth versus Error

In a similar way we can learn to identify God's true lifestyle from a false one by using the absolute standard of scripture. Try comparing the following six areas of life with scripture.

Recreation and Pleasures: We should be able to stop and pray asking God to bless all we do. Test all leisure time by the test in Philippians 4:8–11.

Friends and associates: Love those best who love Christ most. See Exodus 23:2; 2 Corinthians 6:14; James 4:4.

School and Education: Any system of learning that exalts man's wisdom above the Creator's would have to be false. Proverbs 1:7; 1 Corinthians 1:19–31; Matthew 11:28–30.

Diet: Ever since Adam ate forbidden fruit our taste buds have been confused. Taste buds are not a safe guide as to what is good food and what is junk food. 1 Corinthians 3:16; 1 Corinthians 6:19, 20; Proverbs 23:29–35; Ephesians 5:18.

Dress: When how you look is more important than comfort or health, you can be sure you have fallen for a false dress standard. 1 Peter 3:1–5; Proverbs 7:10; 3 John 2; "Therefore, whether you eat or drink, or whatever you do, do all to the glory of God" (1 Corinthians 10:31).

Religions and Churches: Because a person says, "I believe" does not make them a true follower of Jesus. See Matthew 7:21; Isaiah 8:20.

 PRACTICAL PROJECT

Compare a real dandelion to the Sonchus arvensis. Note the differences.

Detecting a Counterfeit

Endurance

Nature Object: Habitat

The dandelion carries its gospel through its seeds to every nation, kindred, tongue, and people the world over. I found a dandelion plant growing at the 8,000-foot level of Whistler Mountain near Jasper, Alberta. This plant grows here because it lives quietly the qualities of endurance. The ten secrets of endurance found in this book are part of this plant's lifestyle. They are part of its very nature. They all work together enabling this plant to grow where almost nothing else can grow. God's love has in it this quality of endurance. "Yes, I have loved you with an everlasting love; therefore with loving kindness I have drawn you" (Jeremiah 31:3).

If we do not resist this enduring love we will be drawn to Him. This divine love was manifested in the humanity of Jesus. He revealed the ten qualities of our dandelion plant by obeying God's ten commandments. "He endured the cross, despising the shame" (Hebrews 12:2).

His love implanted in our hearts will make us loving and kind. Those around us may be rude, hateful, or selfish. The same hatred that has slain the godly from Abel, the first martyr, to the cross, will eventually be directed against any who live God's law of love. Jesus encourages us, "These things I have spoken to you, that in Me you may have peace. In the world you will have tribulation; but be of good cheer, I have overcome the world" (John 16:33).

Dandelions are still blooming around the world in very difficult places. They demonstrate the quality of endurance. Every true flower of Jesus will live this quality of endurance anywhere in our dying world.

 PRACTICAL PROJECT

Find a healthy-looking dandelion plant. Carefully mark the spot where it is growing with a stick stuck into the ground as a marker, so you can find it again. With a pair of scissors cut off the leaves and the flower note the day on the calendar and check your marked spot every day to see how long it takes to grow new leaves and flower. When the flower has grown back, repeat this experiment. How many times will the plant regrow? How does this endurance compare with 2 Corinthians 4:7–11; James 1:2–4; 12–14?

Endurance

Seeing the Big Picture

Nature Object: God's Orchestration

When we look at a dandelion we can see the leaf, stem, flower, and the unseen root all working together to sustain its life. We call this interacting flow 'life.' Each part of the flower is a contributing part of the whole structure of the plant.

Which is more important: the leaf; the flower; the stem; or the root? Each is equally important but not equal in function. Each has its part to play to make the whole happen. It could not have evolved for each part had to be there from the beginning in order that it could live and continue to live.

But the dandelion does not live in this world by itself. There are other plants, trees, birds, and insects that live nearby and they all relate to each other in some kind of ministry. Each has its part to play in the grand orchestration of life.

Which is more important, the bird or the seed? Each needs the other in order that its own life may live. This big picture could not have evolved. Each needed to be in its own place doing its part or none of it could function.

From where did this grand interlocking of life originate? Who was the designer? Who did the construction of each part? Who supplies the power to keep it happening? John 1:3 states: "All things were made through Him, and without Him nothing was made that was made." Verse one tells us this "Him" was the "Word" and verse 14 tells us "the Word became flesh and dwelt among us," and that Word was Jesus. So, the big picture of where the dandelion fits in, is all part of the creative thoughts of Jesus made visible. This wayside "weed" with its 10 secrets of endurance is still quietly sharing its gospel, the good news—God is love!

 PRACTICAL PROJECT

Take a paper and pen and let each family member draw or create his own little world. What would be in it so it could go on living? (Maybe your family tree.) Does each member have his place and work to do? What about how we relate to our street, town, state, country, world and our place in the universe?

Seeing the Big Picture

Subscribe to the Leading Bible-based Nature Journal!

Readers call it, "The Christian answer to National Geographic!"

- Stunning Photography
- Animal & Bird Features
- Creation Science
- Outdoor Travel Adventures
- Gardening Tips
- Youth Photo & Coloring Contests
- Character-building Lessons found in Nature
- Instructional Study Guide
- Even Genesis Cuisine Recipes for healthful living!

UNPLUG and Get Away to Nature & Creation!

4 Quarterly Issues Only $19.95/year–INCLUDES a FREE Digital Subscription
ORDER NOW!
Logon to: **www.CreationIllustrated.com** or Call: **1(800) 360-2732**
or Mail a Check to: **Creation Illustrated, PO Box 141103, Spokane Valley, WA 99214**

The Gospel According to Creation Seminars

Terry McComb, Speaker and Writer with *Creation Illustrated* magazine, has conducted countless character-building, Bible-based seminars that reveal eternal truths through the handiwork of God. The Spiritual messages have a lasting impact on all ages and include black-light chalk drawings with his wife's soft piano artistry in the background.

Pastor McComb has authored more than 50 articles with *Creation Illustrated* magazine and co-authored with his wife Jean, five children's books for parents to study with their children—*Gospel According to a Dandelion; Gospel According to a Blade of Grass; Gospel According to a Snowflake; Gospel According to a Thornless Blackberry;* and *Gospel According to a Tree.*

Available Seminars (available for purchase as a digital download or DVD copy):

"The Creation Story" is a scientific walk through Genesis one. How does each day of the Creation Week reveal its Author and how is this truth relevant to our spiritual walk? A nine-hour seminar from Sunday through Saturday night.

"In His Image" focuses on the wonder of the human body! This nine-hour seminar is a fast-moving study that examines the 12 systems of the body and their amazing designer. Deeply scientific, yet spiritual.

"The Wonder of a Tree" is a nine-hour seminar illustrating how the lifestyle, function, and ways of a tree reveal the ways of its Creator, Jesus Christ.

"Creations Creator" is a five-hour week-end seminar that addresses evolution vs. creation and the truth about Dinosaurs. Topics include: The Cross as Seen in Nature, Worship Him Who Made, Heart Reading Nature, and the Gospel According to a Dandelion power point presentation with music background.

"How to Heart Read Nature" will help viewers learn how to see past the trees and see the Creator. This is a hands-on practical nine-hour seminar that uses the out-of-doors classroom and needs to be in a nature setting. Short on theory and long on active learning.

"The Heavens are Telling" deals with The Gospel According to Astronomy" with plenty of NASA space telescope photos. This nine-hour seminar shows God's ways in outer space to help fill your heart's inner space with His love.

These Seminars can be done by Zoom
To Book a Seminar or order books and DVD's
Call: (250) 547-6696
E-mail: terry@gospelcreation.com
Web site: www.gospelcreation.com
Write: The Gospel According to Creation Seminar
39 Pine Road, Cherryville, British Columbia, Canada V0E 2G3

TEACH Services, Inc.
P U B L I S H I N G

We invite you to view the complete
selection of titles we publish at:
www.TEACHServices.com

We encourage you to write us
with your thoughts about this,
or any other book we publish at:
info@TEACHServices.com

TEACH Services' titles may be purchased in
bulk quantities for educational, fund-raising,
business, or promotional use.
bulksales@TEACHServices.com

Finally, if you are interested in seeing
your own book in print, please contact us at:
publishing@TEACHServices.com
We are happy to review your manuscript at no charge.

www.ingramcontent.com/pod-product-compliance
Lightning Source LLC
Chambersburg PA
CBHW061604170426

43196CB00039B/2970